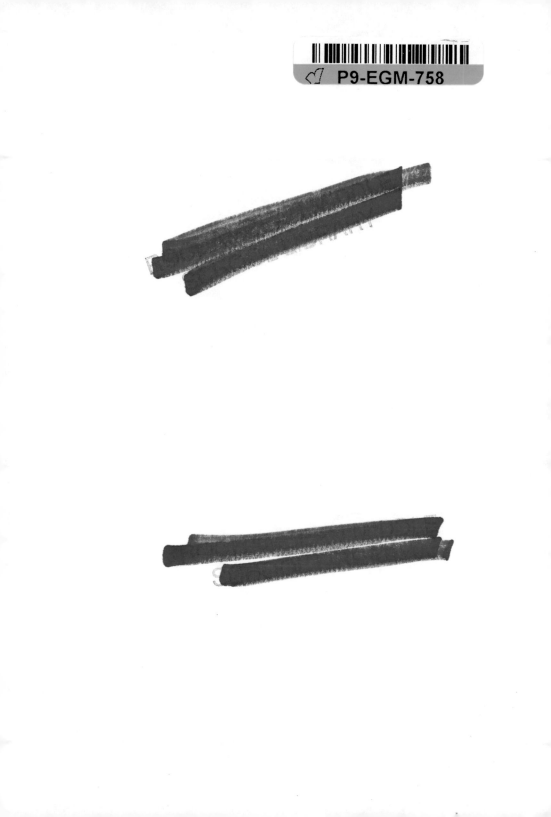

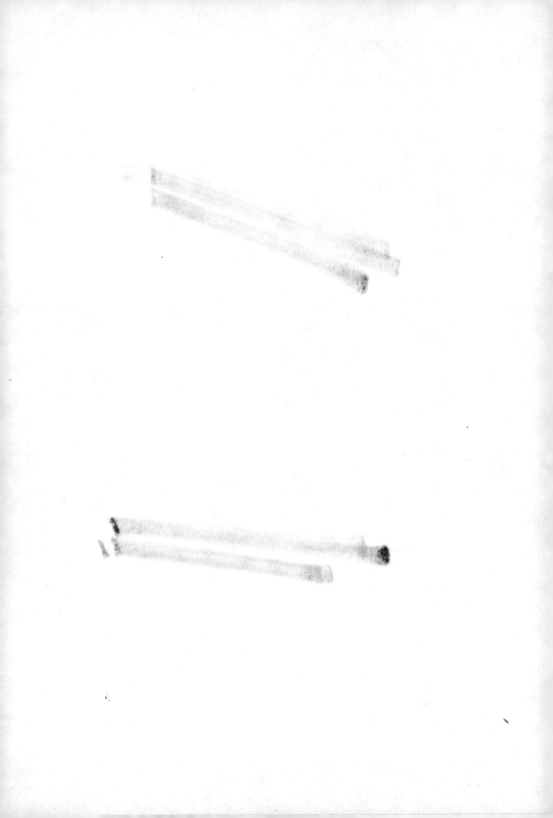

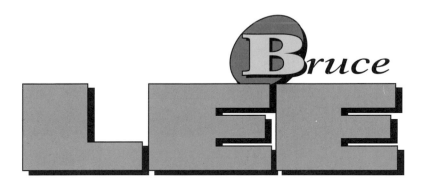

The man who has lived the longest
is not he who has spent the greatest
number of years, but he who has the
greatest sensibility of life.
—*Jean-Jacques Rousseau*

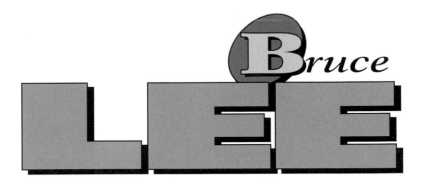

Linda Tagliaferro .

Lerner Publications Company
Minneapolis

To the immortal memories of Bruce Lee and Brandon Bruce Lee

A&E and **BIOGRAPHY** are trademarks of the A&E Television Networks, registered in the United States and other countries.

Some of the people profiled in this series have also been featured in A&E's acclaimed BIOGRAPHY series, which is available on videocassette from A&E Home Video. Call 1-800-423-1212 to order.

This book is available in two bindings:
Library binding by Lerner Publications Company,
  a division of Lerner Publishing Group
Soft cover by First Avenue Editions,
  an imprint of Lerner Publishing Group
241 First Avenue North
Minneapolis, MN 55401 U.S.A.

Website address: www.lernerbooks.com

Library of Congress Cataloging-in-Publication Data

Tagliaferro, Linda.
    Bruce Lee / by Linda Tagliaferro.
      p. cm. — (A&E biography)
    Includes bibliographical references and index.
    Summary: A biography of the well-known actor and martial arts master, Bruce Lee, from his childhood in Hong Kong to his untimely death at the age of thirty-two.
    ISBN 0-8225-4948-4 (lib. bdg. : alk. paper)
    ISBN 0-8225-9688-1 (pbk. : alk. paper)
    1. Lee, Bruce, 1940–1973—Juvenile literature. 2. Actors—United States—Biography—Juvenile literature. 3. Martial artists—United States—Biography—Juvenile literature. [1. Lee, Bruce, 1940–1973. 2. Actors and actresses. 3. Martial artists.] I. Title.
II. Series.
PN2287.L2897T25   2000
791.43′028′092—dc21
[B]   99-26924

Manufactured in the United States of America
2 3 4 5 6 7 – JR – 06 05 04 03 02 01

CONTENTS

Bruce Lee broke racial barriers in Hollywood and inspired an interest in Chinese culture through martial arts.

Chapter **ONE**

THE LETHAL PUNCH

THE AUDIENCE WAS STUNNED. **W**HAT THEY SAW DIDN'T seem possible—but seeing is believing. They watched as a slender but muscular man, barely 5 feet, 7 inches tall and weighing 130 pounds, calmly walked to the center of the stage and positioned his fist near a hulking karate champion's chest. Suddenly, the smaller man pushed his fist forward—just one inch. The taller man seemed to crumple, falling backward across the stage, finally collapsing into a breathless heap on the floor.

The occasion was Ed Parker's first International Karate Championships, held in August 1964 in Long Beach, California. Parker was known as the "Father of American Karate," and he wanted to show the best of the best in his martial arts tournament.

The powerful young man who had effortlessly sent a burly man reeling across the stage—and sent the audience's hearts reeling with him—was Bruce Lee. Born in the United States and raised in Hong Kong, this human dynamo had been asked to demonstrate kung fu skills to an audience that was unfamiliar with the art.

After his impressive demonstration, there were few people in the audience who would ever forget Bruce Lee. One particular spectator, Hollywood hairdresser Jay Sebring, would eventually help make Lee the most famous martial artist and action-movie hero in the world.

Sebring remembered Lee's astounding moments on stage and later raved about his accomplishments to William Dozier. Dozier, one of Sebring's clients, was a television producer who created *Batman* and other television shows. When Dozier saw footage of Lee's demonstration, he called the twenty-four-year-old in for a screen test. He hoped to cast Lee in a proposed television series, *Number One Son*. The show was never created, but the audition led to another part for Lee, in a television series called *The Green Hornet*, which aired in the 1960s.

This part led to others, including movie roles. Eventually, Bruce Lee became the greatest martial arts superstar ever. By the time he died suddenly at age thirty-two, he had achieved everlasting fame. In a little more than three decades, Bruce Lee achieved more than most people who live twice that long.

Lee was the first Asian actor to star in a major American film. He broke racial barriers in Hollywood and inspired an interest in Chinese martial arts and culture in the United States. He paved the way for action-movie stars like Jean-Claude Van Damme, Steven Seagal, Arnold Schwarzenegger, and Jackie Chan, among others.

Bruce Lee was best known as a martial artist and a movie star, but he was much more than that. He was deeply loved by his family. He had lifelong friends on two continents, and he believed strongly in a sensible philosophy of life that inspired those around him. He touched the lives of his friends and family not only while he lived but also after his death.

More than twenty-five years after Bruce Lee's death, he lives on in classic motion pictures such as *Enter the Dragon,* considered by many to be the greatest martial arts movie ever made. Scores of martial arts schools around the world display posters of Bruce Lee. Ask the average person to name a kung fu star, and the answer will invariably be Bruce Lee.

The invincible spirit of Bruce Lee lives on in every martial artist who overcomes mental and physical obstacles to achieve perfection. His spirit lives on in his family and in all those who were fortunate enough to know the genuine human being behind the legend.

Bruce's parents were visiting the United States when he was born. Bruce's mother, Grace, gave birth to him in the Chinatown section of San Francisco, California.

Chapter **TWO**

HOUR OF THE DRAGON

BRUCE LEE WAS BORN IN THE BEST OF YEARS AND the best of hours. The Chinese view dragons not as terrifying creatures but rather as symbols of extraordinary power and good fortune. So it was viewed as a double stroke of good luck when a baby boy was born to the Lee family on November 27, 1940, the Chinese Year of the Dragon, during the Hour of the Dragon, between six and eight o'clock in the morning. According to Chinese astrology, children born in a dragon year will possess great strength and achieve the high goals that they set for themselves.

The boy's proud father was Lee Hoi Chuen (the Chinese place the family name first, then the given name), and his mother was Grace, a beautiful woman

Bruce's parents, Grace Lee and Lee Hoi Chuen

of Chinese and German descent. The couple lived in Hong Kong, which was a British colony at that time but has since become part of China.

Mr. Lee, a popular actor with the Cantonese Opera Company, often traveled abroad. In 1940 Grace accompanied him on a tour of several cities in the United States. So it happened that Grace gave birth to their son in the Jackson Street Hospital in San Francisco's Chinatown section.

In Chinese tradition, naming a baby is of the utmost importance. Chinese families believe a baby's name will affect his or her future.

Chinese babies are first given temporary names, called milk names, to confuse evil spirits that steal children. Mrs. Lee had previously given birth to another baby boy who had died shortly after he was born. So the family was very concerned about picking a milk name that would protect the new baby. They decided to call him Sai Fon, or Little Phoenix (the phoenix is a mythical bird). Sai Fon is a girl's name, and Chinese tradition says that calling a boy by a girl's name will confuse evil spirits.

The baby's real name was Jun Fan, which means "to arouse or shake the foreign countries." A nurse who attended the birth also chose an English name, Bruce, for the baby. Because Hong Kong was a British colony, most children in Hong Kong, including Bruce's brothers and sisters, had both English and Chinese names. The family did not use Bruce's English name until many years later, however.

When Bruce was three months old, the Lee family returned home to Hong Kong. There, Bruce joined his older brother, Peter, and two older sisters, Phoebe and Agnes. Mrs. Lee later gave birth to another son, Robert. The family lived in an apartment at 218 Nathan Road in the Kowloon section of Hong Kong.

When Mr. Lee's brother passed away, his widow and five children moved into the already crowded residence on Nathan Road. The apartment, located on the second floor of a building with a row of shops on the street level, consisted of a living room, two bedrooms,

This piece of jewelry, left, symbolizes the phoenix, a fabled bird from Greek mythology. Bruce's parents at first called him Sai Fon, which means "Little Phoenix."

and only one bathroom. In addition to Bruce's many relatives and a maid, the apartment was home to assorted birds, fish, cats, and dogs.

THE LITTLE DRAGON IN HONG KONG

Located in the tropics, at the southeastern tip of China, Hong Kong has a hot and damp climate. In spring and summer, typhoons—violent tropical storms—sweep the city with heavy winds and rain. Baby Bruce's first encounter with Hong Kong was not a pleasant one. The relentless heat and humidity made him sick.

Although Bruce did not start out as a strong child, he was certainly filled with life as he grew up. The Lee family nicknamed him Mo Si Ting, which means "never sits still," because he had boundless energy. He was constantly talking and moving.

Bruce couldn't even lie still when he was sleeping. He sometimes had nightmares, and his sister Agnes occasionally noticed him climbing down from the top of his bunk bed in the middle of the night to take an unsteady walk around the apartment—even though he was sound asleep.

The family soon learned that the only way to get this perpetual motion machine to stop moving and talking was to give him a book. Young Bruce was an avid reader, and he often stayed up half the night poring over the pages of a new book. Grace Lee was concerned that so much reading contributed to her son's vision problems. From an early age, Bruce was severely nearsighted and needed to wear glasses. (Later in life, he wore contact lenses in public.)

When he wasn't reading or roaming around, he was busy thinking up practical jokes. He once offered his sister Phoebe a book, recommending it highly. When she opened the cover, the book gave off an electric shock. Phoebe cried out in pain, while her mischievous tormentor ran off laughing.

Another time, Bruce rearranged all the furniture at the entrance to the family's apartment. When the maid came home late that night, she struggled in the dark through an unfamiliar maze of chairs and tables, until she finally reached the light in the middle of the room. Grace Lee had to force herself not to laugh when the maid complained about Bruce's antics.

But despite Bruce's devilish streak, his heart was kind. One day, Grace saw her son become agitated as he looked out the living room window in their home. Without stopping to give his mother an explanation, Bruce raced out the door and onto the street below. When Grace peered out the window, she spied her son gently guiding a poor blind man, because no one else had stopped to help him.

Life in the Fragrant Harbor

The name Hong Kong means "fragrant harbor." One of the finest harbors in the world, Hong Kong delights residents and tourists alike with a colorful array of foreign ships, as well as traditional Chinese boats called sampans and junks. Ferries weave in and out of the harbor, which is as crowded with boats and ships as the city's streets are packed with people.

Also known as "the Queen of Exotic Cities" and "the Pearl of the Orient," Hong Kong is a city of contrasts. It has long been renowned for its fine shopping and financial districts. It has sections with extraordinary beauty and wealth, as well as pockets of misery and poverty.

Throughout the bustling city, aromas of delicious food from restaurants fill the air, along with the smell

Bruce is pictured here with his brothers and sisters. From left to right: *Phoebe, Bruce, Agnes, and Peter. Robert is in the front row.*

of garbage rotting in the damp heat. Crowds of people swarm everywhere. Others sit along the street playing mah-jongg, a Chinese game played with tiles. The clacking sounds of the tiles mingle with the noise of voices and traffic.

From the 1840s to 1997, the city of Hong Kong was a British colony. Although most of the citizens were Chinese, they were often looked down upon by their

The city of Hong Kong lies in the tropics at the southeastern tip of China.

colonial rulers. The Chinese were frequently treated unfairly, and the best jobs went to the British minority.

Shortly after Bruce was born, World War II brought other foreign oppressors to the city. From 1941 to

1945, Japanese troops occupied Hong Kong, and they too treated the Chinese poorly. It is easy to understand why many of the films that Bruce went on to make explore the themes of foreign domination and prejudice against the Chinese.

Bruce in his teenage years

Chapter **THREE**

THE LITTLE DRAGON

BECAUSE HIS FATHER WAS IN THE CANTONESE
Opera Company, Bruce grew up surrounded by people
in the entertainment industry. In fact, when he was
just a few months old, he appeared in a movie called
Golden Gate Girl, which was filmed in San Francisco.
Bruce was simply carried onto the set and carried off
again, but this appearance marked the start of his
many film performances as a child.

Back in Hong Kong, Lee Hoi Chuen, Bruce's father,
acted in several supporting roles in a lengthy series of
films about a real Chinese folk hero and martial
artist, Wong Fei Hung. Young Bruce enjoyed watching
his father on the sets of these and other films.

When Bruce was six, the director of one of Hoi

Chuen's films was so impressed by the expressive child that he offered Bruce a role in an upcoming movie, *The Birth of Mankind*. During the next twelve years, Bruce appeared in more than twenty other motion pictures, including *Kid Cheung*, the only movie in which he appeared on screen with his father.

In these early movies, both comedies and tragedies, Bruce already showed the vivid emotions and expressive movements that would make him famous as an adult actor. He began thumbing his nose in defiance, a gesture that would later become familiar to audiences when the adult Bruce Lee prepared for an on-screen fight to the death.

Bruce the child actor was billed as Lee Siu Lung, or "Little Dragon Lee." He would be known by this name throughout the Far East for the rest of his life.

FIGHTING ON ROOFTOPS

In 1952, when Bruce was twelve years old, he enrolled in La Salle Academy, a Catholic boys' school. At home Bruce and his family spoke Cantonese, a southern Chinese dialect. Instruction at school was in English.

In the 1950s, Hong Kong was a tough and sometimes dangerous place, filled with street gangs and organized crime. Racial tensions were high in the city, and the mostly Chinese students at La Salle often fought with British students from the nearby King George V School. Bruce often gathered with his schoolmates on the roofs of buildings to fight rivals.

These confrontations were frequent. More and more, Grace Lee found herself trying to hide Bruce's battles from her husband, who had forbidden their son to fight. Hoi Chuen was often out of the country on opera company tours, so it was difficult for him to discipline Bruce when he found his son had disobeyed orders.

Meanwhile, Bruce found school boring and unrewarding, so he sought other outlets for his tremendous energy. Skilled in expressing himself through motion, he took up dancing and became an expert in the cha-cha, a ballroom dance that involves a series of lively steps and shuffles. He even entered cha-cha competitions, and in 1958 he became the cha-cha champion of Hong Kong.

Bruce was the 1958 cha-cha champion of Hong Kong.

KUNG FU FIGHTER

As Bruce continued to fight with other boys, he soon
realized a need for disciplined martial arts training.
Martial arts—ancient Asian self-defense techniques—
take many forms, including karate, judo, and tae kwon
do. Children in Hong Kong often study the Chinese
martial arts of kung fu (or gung fu, as it is pronounced in Cantonese). It is as common among young
people in Hong Kong as baseball and basketball are
in the United States.

According to legend, kung fu began when a Buddhist
monk, Bodhidharma, traveled from India to the Shaolin
Temple in China in the sixth century A.D. There he developed the fighting style that later evolved into kung fu.

There are countless styles of kung fu, and Bruce studied a few of them before deciding on *wing chun*, a style
which stresses simplicity of movement. Wing chun involves self-defense techniques, often blocking an attack
and striking an opponent at the same time. Straightfor-
ward and direct, this martial art is known for its rapid
punches and low kicks.

Although frequently misunderstood as mere punching
and kicking, the martial arts actually aim to bring
greater peace and harmony to human conflict. They
involve the mind and spirit as well as the body. By
studying the martial arts, one learns discipline and self-
examination, which lead to conflict resolution without
violence.

In many ways, wing chun was the greatest influence

Bruce in his parents' home at 218 Nathan Road in Hong Kong

on Bruce Lee's life because it taught him the philosophy behind the arts of combat. He developed a lifelong interest in Asian philosophies such as Taoism, Zen Buddhism, and Confucianism, which form the spiritual basis of the martial arts. Bruce also had a great interest in Western philosophies, which would later help him to develop his own personal philosophy as a human being—not just an Asian person.

MARTIAL ARTS STUDENT

Bruce became a pupil of Yip Man, a renowned wing chun master, and studied with him for five years, typically for four to six hours a day. Yip Man told Bruce to calm his mind and to forget about himself. Bruce learned that the most important tactic was to be aware of his opponent's every movement. "When the opponent expands, I contract, and when he contracts,

Yip Man, Bruce's martial arts instructor, poses for a photograph with eighteen-year-old Bruce.

I expand," Lee's character explained in *Enter the Dragon* (1973). "And when there is an opportunity, I do not hit. It hits all by itself."

While sailing a small boat in Hong Kong harbor one day, Bruce became so angry at himself for not learning wing chun fast enough that he struck the water with his fist. In a flash, he understood that water illustrates the basic principles of the martial arts. "I struck [the water] . . . with all of my might—yet it was not wounded!" he said.

He also saw that when he tried to hold the water in his hands, it dripped through his fingers. He learned that something as soft and fluid as water can actually be strong and impenetrable. He learned that the mind, body, and spirit of a true martial artist had to have the nature of water.

Still pondering these thoughts, Bruce heard a bird flying overhead and caught a glimpse of its fleeting reflection in the water. "Another mystic sense of hidden meaning revealed itself to me," Bruce said. "Should not the thoughts and emotions I had when in front of an opponent pass like the reflection of the bird flying over the water?"

He realized then what his teacher, Yip Man, meant when he spoke of being detached. Bruce concluded it meant "not being without emotion or feeling, but being one in whom feeling was not sticky or blocked."

Bruce later explained that the study of the martial arts ultimately becomes a study of the self. "How in the process of learning how to use my body can I come to understand myself?" he would ask. While he learned not to dwell on his emotions, he also learned not to hide them. He concluded that in order to control himself, he must first accept himself by going with his own nature.

JOURNEY TO AMERICA

Despite the nonviolent goals of his martial arts training, Bruce continued to fight at school and in the streets. Many teachers saw him as a troublemaker, and he was expelled from La Salle Academy.

The last straw for Grace Lee came when Bruce fought a boy from a rival school and knocked out one of the boy's teeth. Mrs. Lee was called down to the police station and asked to sign a paper promising to see to it that her son's unruly conduct improved.

Around this time, Bruce starred in *The Orphan,* a movie in which he played a troubled teenager. The film was extremely popular and brought Bruce to the attention of the Shaw Brothers, the moviemaking giants of Hong Kong at the time. The Shaws wanted Bruce to appear in their movies, and they offered him a contract.

Bruce didn't take the job, however. Grace Lee was so worried about her son's frequent fighting that she decided it was best for Bruce to forget about show business. Since Bruce had been born in the United States, he was a U.S. citizen. He spoke English at school. After attending English schools, many Hong Kong students went on to work and study in English-speaking countries such as Great Britain, the United States, and Australia. Grace and Hoi Chuen decided that Bruce, too, should leave Hong Kong. In 1958, they sent him to live with friends in the United States.

With a piece of paper listing 108 cha-cha steps and $100 in his pocket, Bruce boarded a ship and set out on a two-and-a-half-week voyage across the Pacific Ocean. A stranger returning to his foreign birthplace, the eighteen-year-old was headed for San Francisco, California.

Seventeen-year-old Bruce, top, *in a scene from the movie* The Orphan, *in which he played a troubled teenager*

He must have felt a combination of adventurous excitement mixed with a fear of the unknown. Would he be lonely and long for his family and friends? Would Americans look down on him in the same way that the British did the Chinese in Hong Kong? How long would the one hundred dollars in his pocket last? What would he do when it ran out? As the ship neared San Francisco, young Bruce Lee had no way to know the great future that awaited him in the United States.

Bruce's martial arts ability eventually landed him a role on the American television series, The Green Hornet. *Bruce,* right, *leaps through the air and surprises an unsuspecting villain.*

Chapter FOUR

JUN FAN
RETURNS

SHORTLY AFTER **B**RUCE **L**EE ARRIVED IN **S**AN **F**RANCISCO, the city of his birth, he traveled to Seattle, Washington, to live with Ruby and Ping Chow. Mr. Chow, along with Bruce's father, had been a member of the Cantonese Opera Company in Hong Kong. His wife, Ruby, ran a successful Chinese restaurant in Seattle.

This was a difficult time for Bruce. Skip Ellsworth, a friend of the martial artist, explained that Bruce had thought he was going to be a guest of the Chow family, "but they put him to work [in the restaurant], and he had no alternative but to go along with that." By attending Edison Technical School during the day and working at Ruby Chow's restaurant at night, Bruce eventually received his high school diploma.

He slept in a tiny room above the restaurant and worked as a busboy and a waiter, jobs he found boring and unrewarding. Ellsworth described Bruce's room on the third floor: "It was exactly the same size as a normal closet. He slept on the floor, and the 'desk' that he studied on was a wooden apple box. Bruce kept his clothes folded on the floor next to his bed. There was one bare lightbulb hanging from the ceiling."

Ellsworth described Bruce as an extremely intelligent and generous person who was especially respectful of the elderly. "Whenever he came to my mother's house for lunch, he would stand up every time she walked into the room," Ellsworth said.

One of Bruce's closest friends was Taky Kimura, a Japanese American who was nearly twenty years his senior. "Bruce had all the attributes of a young teenager: the vibrancy and the endless energy," Taky said. "I was about thirty-eight at the time, but when I found out that here was a young man who could tell you jokes one minute and then the next start talking about some great Zen or Taoist master and discuss that wonderful philosophy of the Far East, I said to myself, 'This guy is only half my age, but I have to be around him.'"

FROM STUDENT TO TEACHER

During this time, Bruce began to teach wing chun to his own students. Skip recalls, "We practiced anywhere we could, often in a parking lot after hours and on weekends. At first there were three or four of us, and then eventually there were maybe ten or fifteen."

One day, Bruce gave a martial arts demonstration at Edison Technical School. One spectator was a street fighter and heavyweight boxer named James DeMile. He was amused at the thought of Bruce's moves being effective self-defense, and DeMile challenged the martial artist.

"Bruce asked if I'd like to take a punch at him," DeMile recalls. "I gave it a shot, but I couldn't do anything." Bruce was so quick that he avoided DeMile's kicks and punches seconds before they even reached him. He weaved and ducked out of the way, often immediately countering with a punch or kick of his own.

Bruce found peace in studying the martial arts.

Bruce Lee and Linda Emery were married in 1964.

"Bruce taught me humility in about five seconds," DeMile said. "He completely controlled me."

DeMile immediately became a student of the martial artist. "He was an inspiration," DeMile said, "because of his tenacity and persistence in achieving a dream, regardless of the obstacles."

After high school, Bruce enrolled at the University of Washington in Seattle and studied philosophy. Soon, the dynamic young man attracted a larger following—students who were fascinated by his martial arts skills and wanted to learn them too.

The students met periodically, often on a lawn in a secluded area of the university grounds. Eventually,

Bruce started the Jun Fan Gung Fu Institute. One of his students was a young Chinese woman named Sue Ann Kay. Enthusiastic about her teacher, Sue Ann convinced her friend Linda Emery to join her at Bruce's school.

Linda, a pretty blond woman and former cheerleader, was fascinated by the concepts of self-defense. But she was equally taken with the handsome young instructor. Bruce and Linda started dating, and less than a year later he proposed to her. She accepted, but finding happiness would not be as easy as they had hoped.

In the 1960s, marriages between Caucasians and Asians were looked down upon. Linda came from a British and Swedish American background and had at first hidden her intentions to marry from her family. But they found out anyway and tried to discourage her from marrying Bruce, who didn't seem to them to have very concrete plans for the future. Nevertheless, Linda and Bruce were very much in love, and they were determined to overcome any obstacles to be together.

In 1964, with Taky Kimura as best man, Linda Emery married Bruce Lee in Seattle. The same day, they moved to Oakland, California, near San Francisco, where Bruce opened another martial arts school. His friend and student James Lee was the assistant instructor. In a small building, Bruce trained about twenty-five students. Eventually, Bruce began to develop his own fighting philosophy called Jeet Kune Do.

Bruce and Brandon Lee

On February 1, 1965, Bruce and Linda were blessed with the birth of a son, Brandon Bruce Lee. His Chinese name was Lee Kwok Ho, which means "Lee National Hero." Since Brandon resembled both his parents, Bruce jokingly referred to him as "the only blond-haired, gray-eyed Chinaman in the world." Sadly, just one week after Brandon was born, Bruce Lee's father died, and Bruce returned to Hong Kong for the funeral.

THE ONE-INCH PUNCH

In 1964, the year Bruce and Linda were married, Bruce was invited to give a kung fu demonstration at the first International Karate Championships. The event was organized by Ed Parker, a renowned martial arts instructor whose most famous student was singer Elvis Presley.

It was at this event that Bruce demonstrated his famous one-inch punch. This demonstration would eventually seal his fate as a star. Sitting in the audience was Jay Sebring, a Hollywood hairdresser whose clients included many powerful people in show business.

When William Dozier, an influential producer, mentioned to Sebring that he was looking for a Chinese actor for a new television series, Sebring immediately recommended Bruce Lee. The series was to be called *Number One Son*. It would tell the story of fictional detective Charlie Chan's eldest son, using adventures similar to those seen in James Bond movies.

Ed Parker had filmed Bruce's demonstration, and after one look at the film presentation, Dozier arranged a screen test for Bruce. Footage of the test showed Bruce leaping, kicking, and punching in an astoundingly powerful yet controlled way. Dozier was impressed.

Bruce and Linda anxiously awaited a phone call from the producer, hoping to learn when shooting would begin on the new adventure series. Unfortunately, plans for *Number One Son* fell through—but Dozier could not forget the dynamic actor. In 1966, he asked Bruce to play the role of Kato, a kung fu–fighting chauffeur, in the television series *The Green*

Hornet. Bruce readily accepted and moved with his family to Los Angeles, where the show was produced.

KATO TO THE RESCUE

In *The Green Hornet,* tall and handsome Van Williams plays Britt Reid, a newspaper publisher who is secretly a masked crime fighter. His aide, Kato, drives the *Black Beauty,* a sleek automobile outfitted with rockets, a special remote camera, and other futuristic gadgets for tracking down and capturing criminals.

The television show was based on a radio show written by George W. Trendle in the 1930s. Together with writer Fran Striker, Trendle had previously written *The Lone Ranger.* He decided to make *The Green Hornet* a direct descendant of the masked hero.

On Friday night, September 9, 1966, the first episode of *The Green Hornet* buzzed onto television screens across the United States. Viewers were delighted. As Kato, Bruce dazzled the audience with dramatic kung fu punches and strikes, gravity-defying leaps, and powerful high kicks.

Outside of Chinese communities, kung fu was almost unknown in the United States. Even though Bruce's performances were limited to a few lines, the electrifying fight scenes (that he choreographed himself) made him the main reason that fans tuned into the show week after week.

Viewers were impressed by Bruce's ferocious grace and speed. But camera operators complained that the

Bruce, left, *as Kato and Van Williams as Britt Reid,* right, *in the short-lived television series* The Green Hornet

fight scenes weren't believable. Their cameras simply weren't fast enough to follow Bruce's lightning-quick kicks and punches, so the people he fought seemed to be suddenly collapsing for no reason. To make the fights seem real, the camera operators asked Bruce to slow down his kicks and punches.

Chapter **FIVE**

THE WARRIOR'S SPIRIT

ALTHOUGH *THE GREEN HORNET* HAD A FAITHFUL following, its popularity was far surpassed by another Dozier production, *Batman*. With its boldly colored scenery, dynamic camera angles that mimicked comic-book art, and words like "Pow!" flashing across the television screen, *Batman* attracted a wider audience than the more subtle stories of the dapper crime fighter and his chauffeur.

One *Batman* episode combined the two shows. It featured Batman, the Caped Crusader, and his side-kick, Robin, fighting the Green Hornet and Kato. Even this episode failed to attract a wider audience for *The Green Hornet*. The show was canceled in 1967, after only one season of twenty-six episodes.

After the show's cancelation, Bruce and his family lived in financially stressful times. Daughter Shannon was born on April 19, 1969. Her Chinese name was Lee Heung Ying, which means "Lee Fragrant Crystallization." With a second child to support, Bruce was all the more concerned about securing a steady income for his family.

Work came in the form of small supporting roles in other television series. Bruce played a nonaction role in an episode of *Here Come the Brides* and appeared in episodes of *Blondie* and *Ironside*. He also costarred in "The Way of the Intercepting Fist," an episode in the *Longstreet* television series.

"The Way of the Intercepting Fist" was named for the English translation of Jeet Kune Do, Bruce's personal fighting philosophy. The episode was written specifically for Bruce by Stirling Silliphant, an award-winning screenwriter and a student of the martial artist.

In the show, James Franciscus plays a blind detective who comes to Lee's character to learn how to defend himself from street toughs. The detective soon finds out that there is more to martial arts than just winning. It offers an awareness that connects the body and the mind. Lee's character advises him, "Empty your mind. Be formless, shapeless, like water. Now you put water into a cup, it becomes the cup. . . . Now water can flow or creep or drip or crash. Be water, my friend." He tells the detective to free himself from his ambitious mind. "Like everyone

The Green Hornet *faced tough competition from the* Batman *series, a show produced by the same company.*

else," he explains, "you want to learn the way to win, but never accept the way to lose."

Lee's performance impressed producers so much that "The Way of the Intercepting Fist" was chosen as the first *Longstreet* episode of the season. Bruce was asked to act in a few more episodes.

Bruce acted in a film called *Marlowe* (1969), also written by Stirling Silliphant and starring James Garner as a detective. In a famous scene in the film, Bruce, as the villain Winslow Wong, angrily trashes Marlowe's office with dramatic high leaps and one astounding kick to an overhead light hanging from an eight-foot ceiling.

In addition to acting, Bruce worked as a fight coordinator on movies such as *The Wrecking Crew* and *A Walk in the Spring Rain*, both produced in 1969. Charles Fitzsimons, the former assistant producer of *The Green Hornet*, convinced Bruce that there was also money to be made in giving private martial arts

This memorable scene in Marlowe shows Bruce shattering a light on an eight-foot ceiling with one swift kick.

lessons to celebrities. Bruce enthusiastically took Fitzsimons's advice and soon was charging as much as $275 an hour to stars such as actor Steve McQueen and basketball player Kareem Abdul-Jabbar.

THE TAO OF JEET KUNE DO

In 1970, Bruce suffered a severe physical setback. During his daily morning exercise routine, he didn't warm up his muscles like he usually did. While holding a 125-pound barbell across his shoulders, Bruce bent down and then straightened up again. He felt a slight discomfort in his lower back but thought nothing of it at the time.

Later, the pain got worse, and Bruce sought out medical help. Doctors told him that he had permanently injured the fourth sacral nerve in his back. He was told to rest—and received the shattering news that he would no longer be able to perform strenuous martial arts kicks and punches.

Bruce was never one to give up, and he had read many books on self-motivation. Whenever he had negative thoughts, he imagined writing them down on a piece of paper and mentally burning them. He refused to listen to the doctors' pessimistic words. Instead, he rested in bed for a few months, then stayed home for

Bruce demonstrates one of the basic martial arts positions.

THE ROOTS OF JEET KUNE DO

n 1965, several Chinese martial artists came to Bruce's school. They handed him a scroll that issued a challenge. Because of a history of foreign domination, some Chinese martial artists weren't comfortable with Bruce teaching their fighting secrets to foreigners. They proposed a fight between Bruce and one of the martial artists. If Bruce lost, he would have to stop teaching non-Asians, or else close his school.

Bruce took up the challenge, and within minutes his opponent surrendered. Bruce had won the right to continue teaching. But the fight caused him to reevaluate his fighting style. Why did it take minutes to defeat his opponent, he asked himself, instead of just seconds? From that moment on, he studied the most efficient movements possible and incorporated them into an art he called Jeet Kune Do, which means "the Way of the Intercepting Fist" in Cantonese.

Jeet Kune Do is based on the skills and strategies of hand-to-hand combat. However, Bruce never called his martial art a style. He thought the word implied that certain rules had to be followed. His wife, Linda, explained, "There's a certain degree of freedom in the way Bruce practiced his martial arts because he saw a rigidity in the practice of many martial arts styles—a clinging to what the instructor taught, whether or not it worked for that particular person."

Bruce felt that after learning some fundamentals, students could explore what worked for them as individuals. If a person always relied on the same kick or punch, then an opponent could easily find a way to defeat that style of fighting. Bruce's business card contained the motto, "Using no way as way, having no limitation as limitation," to explain that students could go beyond set patterns. They should learn from experience and intuition, he said, and adapt to the ever-changing situations in real combat.

another three months—reading, writing, and exploring his thoughts on the martial arts.

Bruce was still an avid reader, and his huge collection of books ranged from works on martial arts to writings by philosophers such as the Indian mystic Krishnamurti. He read Norman Vincent Peale's books on the power of positive thinking, and he studied books about Western boxing and fencing. As he rested at home, Bruce also put together notes for his own book, *The Tao of Jeet Kune Do* (*tao* is a Chinese word meaning "way"). The book, which wasn't published until after Bruce's death, explained Bruce's fighting philosophy.

Linda Lee recalls: "[The injury] was a stumbling block that Bruce turned into a stepping stone. It was frustrating at times, but he accepted the necessity for him to heal himself. He allowed his body to heal while his mind was still active. I don't think he ever believed that he would never be doing martial arts again, as the doctors had told him." Indeed, through a combination of rest, willpower, and motivation, Bruce returned to his passionate practice of the martial arts, despite the doctors' predictions.

THE WARRIOR

Bruce often told his wife and friends that he wanted to teach the world more about the Chinese people and to promote racial understanding and equality through motion pictures. He also wanted to make a film called

The Silent Flute, which would explain his martial arts philosophy. Unable to secure financial backing or find a suitable location for filming, Bruce dropped the project.

Bruce pushed forward, however, becoming involved with another project that would educate people about the martial arts. The project was a television series called *The Warrior* that would feature a kung fu artist, a monk from the famed Shaolin Temple in China. In the series, the monk would roam through the American Old West, using his martial arts skills to defend himself against villains on horseback. Bruce helped develop the series, and he also hoped to be its star.

Renamed *Kung Fu,* the show became popular—but not with Bruce Lee as the star. The producers and other decision makers thought Bruce looked "too Chinese." They feared that American television viewers were not ready for an Asian star. Instead, they gave the role to American actor David Carradine and wrote his character as half-Chinese, half-American.

Bruce realized that breaking through the barriers of prejudice in Hollywood would take time and perseverance. He decided to temporarily set his sights on filmmaking in his native Hong Kong. He thought he might have a better chance of building up his reputation as a celebrity there.

Bruce's widow explains, "One of the [ideas] that Bruce led his life by was that you can't always change the things that happen to you, but [what is important

Linda and Bruce with daughter, Shannon

is] how you react to those events. So while Bruce was sorely disappointed at encountering prejudice in Hollywood, he chose to deal with that by creating an opportunity."

Taking his wife, son, and daughter on an airplane to the rolling hills and colorful harbor of Hong Kong, Bruce once again had high hopes for his future across the ocean. Again, he could not predict the tremendous good fortune that awaited him in his native city.

Chapter SIX

FISTS OF FURY

IN 1970, WHEN BRUCE LEE STEPPED OFF THE PLANE at Kai Tak Airport in Hong Kong, he never suspected that he was a known actor in his own hometown. Unknown to Bruce, *The Green Hornet* had been dubbed into Cantonese, renamed *The Kato Show*, and aired on Hong Kong television. The show was a tremendous success, especially after viewers discovered that Bruce Lee was a native of their own city. The show was also a hit in other parts of Asia.

Immediately upon his return, Bruce was bombarded by offers to appear on Hong Kong's most popular television talk shows. During one appearance, Bruce requested that two black-belt karate champions appear with him. He instructed one of the karate champions to hold an air bag in front of him for protection. The second black belt was positioned behind the first. Bruce stood about five feet away from the first man and instructed the second man to catch the first if he fell from Bruce's kick.

The two karate champions never knew what hit them. They never expected such power from such a small distance away. With one kick, Bruce propelled the first man backward. The second man, unable to withstand the force of Bruce's energy, crashed into the stage set behind him. Hong Kong's television viewers had never seen anything like this. Bruce's fame in the city grew even more that night.

THE BIG BOSS

With Bruce's increased popularity in Asia, he started receiving offers from filmmakers. One of the first requests came from Run Run Shaw of Shaw Brothers Studios. Despite the Shaw Brothers' tremendous success in the Asian movie market, their salary offers to film stars were low. Bruce refused to sign a contract unless the studio paid him fairly for his work as an actor.

Shortly after Bruce refused the Shaw Brothers, he got a better offer from a former Shaw employee, Raymond Chow, who had gone off on his own to create Golden Harvest Studios. Bruce signed a contract with Chow, agreeing to make two movies with Golden Harvest.

In July of 1971, Bruce flew to Pak Chong, a remote

Bruce, center, *in a scene from* Fists of Fury

village in Thailand, to film the first movie for Chow. The film was entitled *The Big Boss* in Asia but was released in the United States as *Fists of Fury.* The budget for the movie was small, and a lot of that money was spent on gallons of fake blood for the gory action scenes.

In a letter to his wife, Linda, Bruce complained that meat was scarce in the village where they were filming. Between the heat, humidity, and lack of acceptable food, Bruce lost weight. Mosquitoes buzzed incessantly at night as he tried to sleep in the only hotel in the small Thai village. Cockroaches crawled in and out of the floorboards.

To make matters worse, Bruce sprained his ankle during one of the last fight scenes and had to be driven two hours to Bangkok, Thailand's capital city, to be treated by a doctor. Bruce missed his family so much that he wrote Linda and asked her to send photos. But when filming was over, the movie's success would make all the inconveniences worthwhile.

AN OVERNIGHT SUCCESS

The Big Boss, like many Hong Kong action movies, had a predictable plot. In the movie, Bruce Lee plays a Chinese man named Cheng who moves to Thailand to live and work with relatives. Around his neck he wears a pendant, which symbolizes a promise he made to his mother to keep out of fights.

In the beginning of the movie, Cheng strains to keep from intervening when he sees others start trouble. But midway through the movie, Cheng is finally pushed too far, and he reacts with all the fury of a wild animal. He single-handedly defends himself against Thai thugs, all the while letting off eerie, high-pitched shrieks and moans that frighten his opponents even more.

In October 1971, *The Big Boss* premiered in Hong Kong. Linda and Bruce sat expectantly in the audience, wondering why the other viewers were so quiet. They began to suspect that the viewers were not enjoying the action, but all doubt was removed when "The End" flashed onto the screen. After a brief moment of silence, the audience started cheering and stood up to applaud the raw talent they had witnessed.

What made *The Big Boss* different from other Chinese martial arts films was Bruce Lee's insistence on realism. Traditionally, similar movies centered around Chinese folk heroes who engaged in fights that were more fantasy than plausible action. The fighters, suspended by wires, twirled around in the air with swords, executing impossible leaps and falls. These superhuman action scenes made up the bulk of the movies.

With *The Big Boss*, Hong Kong audiences saw an actor perform realistic moves and powerful yet believable kicks and punches. For the first time ever, Bruce used modern weapons such as knives and chains instead of traditional swords. But mostly he relied on his lethal hands and feet to destroy his enemies. His screen presence was electrifying and more than made up for a trivial plot.

The Big Boss quickly became Hong Kong's best-selling movie, outgrossing *The Sound of Music*, which had previously held the record. Bruce Lee became even more of a sensation. He earned a new nickname—the Fastest Fist in the East.

The Chinese Connection

Now that Bruce was a matinee idol in Hong Kong, his many fans clamored for another film starring their hero. He didn't let them down. Bruce's second movie

Bruce Lee explodes with fury in the dramatic ending of The Chinese Connection.

for Golden Harvest Studios was based on the true story of a martial arts teacher in Shanghai—a city in China—who had been secretly poisoned by the Japanese in the early 1900s. This film was called *Fist of Fury* in Hong Kong and was later released as *The Chinese Connection* in the United States.

One reason for the film's popularity was the anti-Japanese sentiments harbored by Hong Kong residents. Throughout its history, Hong Kong had had a series of unpleasant encounters with Japan. During World War II, the Chinese in Hong Kong suffered greatly from the Japanese occupation, and this period of foreign domination had not been forgotten. Bruce Lee had personally felt the hardships of foreign rule as he was growing up.

In *The Chinese Connection,* Japanese martial artists barge into the Ching Wu martial arts school. The arrogant foreigners carry a framed sign that reads, "The Chinese are the sick men of Asia." They try to bait the students into a fight, and Bruce Lee, as Chen, is ready to pounce on the insulting visitors. But another student reminds him that their now-deceased *sifu,* or teacher, had always preached a doctrine of peace and nonviolence.

The audience sees an inflamed Bruce Lee, his face contorted with rage and resentment, holding himself back as he remembers the words of his revered master. The Japanese villains gloat and mock the Chinese students on their way out.

Later in the movie, Chen cannot contain himself any longer—he has been pushed to the breaking point. Silent but with deadly determination, he enters the Japanese martial arts academy and, in a breathtaking show of strength, he single-handedly takes on the entire school.

With lethal grace, he finishes off the last of the Japanese students and announces, "The Chinese are not the sick men of Asia." He forces two students to eat the scroll carrying those words and warns them, "This time you're eating paper . . . the next time it's going to be glass!"

This particular scene struck a deep chord with Chinese audiences. Sneaking into a Hong Kong movie theater, Bruce once sat in the back and secretly observed the audience reaction. As Chen spoke his vengeful lines, restoring the self-respect of his countrymen, the audience went wild with emotion and national pride. They shrieked and applauded the Chinese hero.

Another scene in *The Chinese Connection* brought out the same mood in the audience. When Chen tries to gain admission to a park, a burly East Indian guard bars his way. Looking askance at Chen, the guard growls, "You're the wrong color." He points to a sign that reads, "No dogs and Chinese allowed." (This sign is said to have actually existed in Shanghai in the early 1900s.)

When a Japanese man taunts Chen, telling him to pretend to be a dog and crawl into the park, the insulted martial artist reacts by attacking the sarcastic man. Chen ends the tense, emotional scene by leaping into the air and smashing the hateful sign into pieces with one spectacular kick.

Ticket sales for *The Chinese Connection* topped even the record-breaking numbers for *The Big Boss,* and Bruce Lee's fame spread further throughout the Far East. Whenever he walked out on the streets of Hong Kong, crowds of adoring fans mobbed him and asked for his autograph. He requested an unlisted telephone number and, at times, even went out in disguise to keep fans at bay.

THE FASTEST FIST IN THE EAST

 ruce Lee always amazed people with his incredible speed. Once during his *Green Hornet* days, Bruce was interviewed by John Owen of the *Seattle Post-Intelligencer,* a newspaper in Washington State. After the interview, Bruce gave the reporter a demonstration of some lightning-fast punches and kicks.

As Owen was about to leave, Bruce offered to test the man's reflexes. He put a dime into the reporter's palm and said he was going to try to grab it. Owen was ready, and when Bruce reached out, the reporter clutched the coin tightly.

The self-assured writer grinned when Bruce complimented him on his reflexes and asked to see the dime. As Owen opened his clenched fist, he suddenly lost the smug smile on his face. There was now a penny in his hand, and a smiling Bruce showed him the dime that he had stolen out from under his nose.

Others attested to Lee's swift reflexes. When Lalo Schifrin, composer of the theme music for *Enter the Dragon,* met Bruce, he felt a soft breeze near his nose. Bruce had kicked and purposely missed Schifrin's face by a fraction of an inch. Another time, *Return of the Dragon* actor Jon T. Benn recounted how Bruce knocked just the ashes off the cigar in Benn's mouth with one precise, rapid kick.

RETURN OF THE DRAGON

Now that Bruce's status as a star was firmly established in Hong Kong and the rest of Asia, he did
something that no Hong Kong actor had ever done before. He not only asked for more money, he also de-
manded more control over the quality of his movies.

Because of his popularity and the demand for more
films with the Asian superstar, Bruce had no problem
getting producer Raymond Chow to agree to his requests. In addition, Bruce insisted on better wages
and working conditions for actors and film crews in
Hong Kong. This effort made him extremely popular
with workers in the film industry.

In 1972, Bruce embarked on a project that he wrote,
cast, produced, directed, and acted in. The film was
called *Way of the Dragon* but was later known as *Return
of the Dragon* (because it was released in the United
States after Bruce's final movie, *Enter the Dragon*).

With this movie, Bruce attempted a number of revo-
lutionary firsts for a Hong Kong moviemaker. Aside
from his tremendous involvement in all aspects of the
film's creation, he took the crew to Italy to shoot most
of the scenes. *Return of the Dragon* marked the first
time that a Hong Kong movie was filmed in Europe.

Bruce brought in non-Asian talent to give the film
even more of an international flavor. One actor was
Chuck Norris, the famed American karate champion
who has since been known for his many action

Chuck Norris and Bruce fight it out in a scene from Way of the Dragon.

movies and his starring role in the television series *Walker, Texas Ranger*. Norris was relatively unknown as an actor in the early 1970s, but he had won nearly every major karate championship in the late 1960s.

In a dynamic, unforgettable scene in *Return of the Dragon*, Chuck Norris as the evil Colt and Bruce Lee as the naive Chinese country boy Tang Lung face off in the ruins of the Colosseum, the huge amphitheater in Rome where fearless gladiators fought to the death in ancient times.

At the beginning of this classic scene, Tang Lung stubbornly clings to his style of kung fu and consequently starts to lose as Colt bombards him with lethal kicks and punches. Suddenly, realizing that he must adapt to the situation and fight more fluidly, Tang Lung—reflecting Bruce Lee's philosophy—starts to "be like water." Switching tactics, he forgets his own ego and begins to anticipate Colt's every move, reacting instantaneously and without thinking. Colt is killed, and a somber Tang Lung takes his opponent's jacket and covers his lifeless figure in a gesture of dignity and admiration for the fallen fighter.

Kareem Abdul-Jabbar, right, *who was at one time a student of Bruce's, battles Bruce in* Game of Death.

GAME OF DEATH

In 1972, the same year that *Return of the Dragon* became a hit, Bruce started work on another movie, *Game of Death.* Inspired by a series of Bruce's dreams, the story centers around a man, played by Bruce, who searches for a stolen treasure. He learns that the prized possession is located on the top floor of a many-storied pagoda in Korea. But each floor is guarded by a feared martial artist, each with his own lethal brand of hand-to-hand and foot-to-face combat.

The final scenes, those in the pagoda, were filmed first. They feature some of the world's finest martial artists. In the movie, the first floor is guarded by a character played by Bruce's student Dan Inosanto. He was a master at the Filipino martial art of *escrima*, which includes stick-fighting techniques. Inosanto was also adept at using the nunchaku, a weapon made of two wooden dowels connected by a length of cord or chain. In the hands of an expert, this weapon can inflict deadly strikes.

On the next floor, Bruce's character encounters Chi Hon Tsoi, a master of *hapkido*—a Korean martial art. Each man tests Bruce's ability to adapt to a different fighting style. The highlight of these scenes is Bruce's face-off with professional basketball player Kareem Abdul-Jabbar. At seven feet, two inches, Bruce's former student presented a gigantic challenge for the five-foot, seven-inch Lee. Once again, Bruce's character fights with fluidity, adjusting to the unknown style of his enormous opponent. He emerges from the pagoda undefeated.

Shortly after these scenes were filmed, Bruce was offered a starring role in an American movie produced by Warner Brothers. He knew that this role could catapult him into stardom in the United States, so he decided to begin work on the movie and return to *Game of Death* after its completion.

The name of the American motion picture was *Enter the Dragon*, and it was destined to become the all-time martial arts classic. But, as tragic fate would have it, Bruce would not live to see the film released.

Chapter SEVEN

ENTER THE DRAGON

THE MUSCLE-BOUND HERO GLIDES THROUGH A MAZE of mirrors. Fleeting images of his stealthy opponent appear all around him, then abruptly disappear, like fireflies on a summer night. Suddenly, a bear's claw attached to the villain's stump of an arm slashes at the hero's back. He swings around wildly, only to catch a glimpse of his opponent, vanishing once again within the mirrored maze.

Confused and frustrated, the bare-chested hero suddenly remembers the words of his kung fu master at the Shaolin Temple: "Your enemy has only images and illusions behind which he hides his true motives. Destroy the image and you will break the enemy." Filled with inspiration, the hero swings at the mirrors, and his powerful punches smash the glass panels into patterns that look like jagged spider webs.

The villain can no longer hide behind the false images, and he succumbs to the hero's brutal fury. With one ferocious kick, the hero sends his opponent reeling backward into a spear that juts out of a mirrored wall and to his final defeat.

The hero is Bruce Lee, and his adversary is the mysterious Han (played by Chinese actor Shih Kien),

Bruce's performance helped to make Enter the Dragon *one of the classic martial arts films of all time.*

a heartless villain who has betrayed his martial arts training to become a criminal. This is the climactic scene of *Enter the Dragon,* considered the greatest martial arts movie ever made.

Enter the Dragon was coproduced by Warner Brothers and Concord Productions, a company set up in Hong Kong by Bruce Lee and Raymond Chow. The movie was the first such collaboration of an established American studio and a Hong Kong studio. It was the first film to star an Asian actor and catapult him to international fame. It featured well-known American martial artists such as karate champions Jim Kelly and Bob Wall, Okinawan hapkido champion Angela Mao Ying, and Yang Sze, now known as Bolo Yeung, a karate champion of Asia.

The movie was shot in Hong Kong with an American and Chinese crew. Although the budget of six hundred thousand dollars was much higher than that of most Hong Kong action movies, it was well under the amounts usually spent on American movies at the time. To Warner Brothers, six hundred thousand dollars was very little, about what the studio normally spent on a pilot—or sample episode—of a TV show. So Warner Brothers didn't mind taking a chance on what they considered the risky business of featuring an Asian star.

Enter the Dragon revolves around Bruce Lee's character, also called Lee, who is sent by a Mr. Braithwaite from an international agency to gather information

about the notorious Han, a Shaolin monk who has left
the noble path of the renowned martial arts temple in
China. Instead of using his knowledge for the better-
ment of humankind, Han runs a drug-trafficking trade
on an island in the middle of the South China Sea.

Advertising a martial arts tournament on the island
every three years, Han recruits partners in crime from
the top champions who come to compete. Lee agrees
to go to the tournament when he realizes that Han's
ruthless bodyguard, Oharra, had once stalked Lee's
own sister. She had committed suicide rather than
allow the bodyguard to disgrace her. So Lee has a personal as well as a professional motive for revenge.

John Saxon as Roper and Jim Kelly as Williams are
tournament participants who also try to penetrate the
hidden secrets of the ominous island fortress of Han.
The martial artists are treated to a sumptuous banquet
with exotic entertainment, but Roper wonders if they
are "being fattened up for the kill."

Lee sneaks out of his room at night and discovers an
underground opium-processing plant. When the evil
Han gets word that someone has been prowling
around in the darkness, he mercilessly orders his
guards killed for their failure to keep the competitors
imprisoned within their rooms.

At the tournament, Lee fights the brutal Oharra
(played by Bob Wall). When Han's bodyguard realizes
that he is on the verge of defeat, he desperately at-
tempts to attack Lee with two broken bottles. Lee is

too fast for him, however, and with one superhuman leap, he kicks Oharra to death. At the sight of the fallen bodyguard, Han rises and announces, "Oharra's treachery has disgraced us all."

When everyone has retired to their rooms for the night, Lee solves the riddle of Han's island. He enters secret passages, observing the opium operation, women being forcefully addicted to drugs, and many lost souls entrapped in dungeons.

He lets loose a deadly cobra that he had captured on the grounds. When some of Han's men scatter to escape from the venomous snake, Lee manages to send a message by radio to Mr. Braithwaite. Han's savage guards rush after him, and Lee astounds everyone by his extraordinary fighting with double sticks, lethal Chinese weapons. Next, he threatens them by twirling the deadly nunchaku.

Just as he is about to make his escape, Lee finds himself trapped in a small enclosure—steel doors have crashed down on all sides. Like a true martial artist, Lee sits down in a meditative, cross-legged position, slings his nunchaku around his neck, closes his eyes, and waits patiently, aware of his surroundings all the while.

The next day, the tournament continues, and Han orders Roper to fight with Lee, who has been released from the enclosure. Roper refuses, and out of spite Han orders him to battle with the heartless guard Bolo. When Roper kills the brawny bodyguard, an enraged Han instructs his men to attack Roper and

Lee. Before Han's men can follow his orders, they are attacked by hundreds of prisoners from the underground dungeon, set free by Mei Ling, a female agent who was also sent to the island by Braithwaite.

A furious battle follows between Han's men and Lee, Roper, and other combatants. Lee pursues an escaping Han into the hall of mirrors, a chase that ends in the villain's death. With the battle already won, Braithwaite's agency sends soldiers, who arrive on the island in helicopters long after they are needed.

CREATING A CLASSIC

The filming of *Enter the Dragon* was not without problems. To begin with, many members of the Chinese crew did not speak English, and almost none of the Americans spoke Chinese. Often, one person who spoke two languages would translate, but sometimes meanings would get lost in the translation.

When it was time to film the scenes with the mirrored maze, more problems developed. To hide the camera, the crew constructed a small room covered with mirrors within the maze. Producer Paul Heller explained, "We had to have tons of lights, and it was like a furnace in there." Heller asked crew members to install a fan on top of the set, but no one was sure who should do it. "That's when we went to Bruce, and with just one word from him, everybody sprang into action and it was done," said Heller. "The Chinese crew adored him and would do anything for him."

Another problem arose when Bruce handled the cobra. Normally, this type of snake sinks its fangs into victims and kills them with its deadly venom. The crew on the movie had purchased a snake with its venom sacs removed, and this wise move prevented a tragic accident. To rouse the sleeping snake when it was taken out of a bag, Bruce once hit it on the top of its head. Suddenly, the annoyed cobra sank its fangs into Bruce's flesh. Although it was not a lethal bite, it was extremely painful.

Because *Enter the Dragon* was filmed on a relatively small budget, supplies were not always readily available.

The climactic scene of Enter the Dragon *takes place in a maze of mirrors.*

The sturdy-looking walls in the dungeon scene, for instance, were created from mud spread onto chicken wire and mixed with pieces of wood.

Screenwriter Michael Allin's original script called for a scene with Han and Roper talking on the villain's grounds. To underscore Han's wicked nature, the scene was to take place by a sinister pond, ruled by an evil black swan. The crew searched high and low, but no such swan could be found, and the scene had to be deleted from the script.

REAL RISKS ON THE SET

Some of the actors had unpleasant experiences during filming, ranging from mild discomfort to near tragedy. In one scene, which reflects the philosophy underlying the martial arts, Peter Archer's character, Parsons, tries to bait Lee into fighting with him on a junk headed for Han's island. Lee calmly resists. But when the bully persists and aggressively grabs Lee's arm, the calmer, self-assured martial artist agrees to show him "the art of fighting without fighting."

Lee convinces Parsons to row to a nearby island with him for an all-out fight. The impatient fighter agrees, quickly hops into a small rowboat, and waits for Lee to join him. But as Parsons settles into the boat, he is surprised to find that Lee has no intention of following him. Lee allows the smaller boat to float out in the water while he calmly holds a connecting rope. He warns Parsons that if he tries to climb back

BEHIND THE SCENES

here was more than meets the eye (and ear) in the creation of *Enter the Dragon*. Here are some little-known facts about the martial arts classic:

- Whenever Bruce Lee lands a lethal kick or punch in the movie, the audience hears a resounding smack and sees the opponent fall. What you don't see is Bruce Lee just missing his human target by only a fraction of an inch.

- To make those attacks sound like the real thing, sound engineers snapped chicken bones next to a microphone. They also created the sounds of lethal blows by hitting melons with thin bamboo rods or squashing them with hammers.

- Michael Allin's original screenplay was called *Blood and Steel*. The title then went through several changes. Producers almost settled on *Han's Island*, but Bruce suggested *Enter the Dragon*. Because Bruce was known in Asia as the Little Dragon, he knew the name would carry a greater meaning for Far Eastern audiences.

- Where did the name of British agent Mr. Braithwaite come from? Screenwriter Michael Allin explained, "[Producer] Fred Weintraub came up with that name early on. He was looking for something to make the character really British, and [Braithwaite] sounds like someone who's holding his breath while waiting to hear what's happened."

into the junk, he will release the rope altogether. This made a wonderful scene in the movie. But in real life, Peter Archer nearly drowned in the South China Sea as water filled the small vessel.

The greatest risks, however, were in the fighting scenes. Bruce often sprang into the air to give lethal and impressive kicks to his screen enemies. But during those scenes, Bruce always stopped short of touching his human targets by a fraction of an inch so that no one got hurt. "I never met anybody in my life who worked so hard and cared so much," noted producer Paul Heller. "Think about his kicks. It looks as if he hit somebody right in the head, but he had to stop and hold back in the middle of it. It's the most amazing bit of athletics that you can imagine."

During one of these kicks, a stuntman was standing in the wrong position. In order not to injure this man, Bruce drew back so suddenly and forcefully that he pulled a muscle in his groin. During another scene, Bruce sent a powerful kick to actor Bob Wall, propelling him back so forcefully that Wall broke the arms of a man on the set waiting to catch him.

The most serious accident occurred when Bruce and Bob Wall's characters face off at the tournament. During rehearsals, Bruce spun around toward his opponent, and Bob Wall dropped a broken glass bottle just in time. But during the actual filming, Wall's timing was off and he held onto the bottle. As a result, when Bruce turned, he gashed his hand on the glass and

Although Bruce and Bob Wall execute this scene without any problem in Enter the Dragon, *filming it wasn't simple. During actual filming, Wall's timing was off and he held onto the glass bottle too long, causing Bruce to cut his hand. Bruce went to the hospital for stitches and filming was stopped for days.*

needed twelve stitches. All filming had to be stopped for four days.

Sudden Collapse

Despite the obstacles in filming, *Enter the Dragon* was finally on its way to completion. But on May 10, 1973, Bruce suffered another major setback. Working in a dubbing room (the studio where sound is added to a film after shooting) without air-conditioning, in Hong Kong's intense humidity and heat, Bruce felt faint, so he went to the men's room.

Suddenly, the ground seemed to give out from under him, and he collapsed. Crew members took him to a hospital. Bruce was unconscious and had difficulty breathing. Doctors detected a swelling of the brain, a life-threatening condition, and gave him medicine. Luckily, Bruce regained consciousness and left the hospital, but everyone who knew him was badly shaken.

Bruce later flew back to the United States, where his own doctor examined him but could find no cause for the collapse. The doctor sent him home with the optimistic message that Bruce was as physically fit as a teenager. Relieved, Bruce returned to Hong Kong and awaited the August release of his movie.

On July 20, in the home of a costar who was reviewing the *Game of Death* script with him and Raymond Chow, Bruce complained of a severe headache. His costar gave him a prescription pill, Equagesic, and Bruce went to lie down until the headache passed. He never woke up.

When no one could wake him, Raymond Chow called an ambulance, and Bruce was rushed to Queen Elizabeth Hospital. Although doctors tried to revive him, nothing could be done. Bruce Lee was pronounced dead. The cause of death was cerebral edema, or swelling of the brain. Doctors said the swelling was caused by a rare allergic reaction to the pill Bruce had taken.

At the height of his film career and poised for international stardom, Bruce Lee had passed away. Many fans refused to believe that a perfect specimen of muscle-bound masculinity could expire so suddenly. Rumors spread that he had been poisoned or killed by the Chinese Mafia. Some people speculated that a rival filmmaker like Run Run Shaw had ordered Bruce's death. Still others believed that he was alive but in hiding from intrusive fans.

Another rumor said that Bruce had been felled by *dim mak*—"the vibrating palm"—an alleged death touch. Supposedly administered by a martial arts henchman, dim mak works its fatal effects by delayed reaction on its victim.

With the newspapers printing accounts of secret plots and murderous intentions, Linda, Bruce's widow, announced her conviction that she held no one responsible for her husband's death. As the rumors swirled, the fact remained that Bruce Lee was gone forever at the age of thirty-two.

Thousands of mourners crowded the streets for Bruce's funeral in Hong Kong. Later, a group of family and friends attended his burial in Seattle, Washington, at Lake View Cemetery.

The world was shocked and saddened by the sudden death of Bruce Lee. Over twenty-five years after his death, fan clubs and organizations dedicated to Bruce Lee's memory still exist around the world.

Chapter EIGHT

AFTER
BRUCE LEE

AFTER THE TRAGIC EVENT ON JULY 20, 1973, THE
martial arts world mourned the loss of its greatest
actor and beloved idol. Fan mail about Bruce Lee
poured into magazines like *Inside Kung Fu* and
Fighting Stars, and it continues to this day, many
years after the death of the Little Dragon. *Enter the
Dragon*, released in August 1973, was a huge success.

Movie producers, both in Hong Kong and the United
States, scrambled to find a replacement for Bruce Lee,
but that proved to be an impossible task. No one had
the charisma, talent, speed, power, good looks, and
emotional depth to match the man fans called the
King of Kung Fu.

A whole slew of kung fu movies came out shortly

after Lee's death. These combative melodramas featured kung fu practitioners with stage names concocted to remind fans of the masterful martial artist who was gone forever. Names like Bruce Li, Bruce Le, Bruce Liang, Dragon Lee, and even Myron Bruce Lee flashed across movie screens in an attempt to draw the audiences who longed to see their departed hero once more.

Some producers cranked out kung fu films with purposely misleading titles such as *Bruce Lee Fights Back from the Grave*, *The Dragon Dies Hard*, and others with the words *dragon, game,* and *fists* woven into the titles. No actor ever came close to achieving Bruce Lee's status, although many tried.

GAME OF DEATH

Bruce Lee was gone, but Golden Harvest still had footage of the martial arts master in his uncompleted movie, *Game of Death*. Raymond Chow pondered what to do with the combat scenes featuring Bruce pitted against martial arts greats such as Dan Inosanto and basketball legend Kareem Abdul-Jabbar.

Chow decided he could never film the movie the way Bruce had intended it, so he had an entirely different story written around the existing footage. Three Bruce Lee look-alikes were enlisted to fill in the action. Chinese actor Chen Yao Po replaced Bruce Lee's character in most of the acting scenes, and Kim Tai Chung, a Korean martial arts master, took over for the fighting scenes. A third stand-in, Yuen Biao, performed the more demanding acrobatic stunts.

The new story centered around a character named Billy Lo. In an attempt to explain why the three replacements do not look exactly like Bruce Lee, Billy is shot in the face early in the movie. At first, his wounded face is bandaged. Later, the character appears in a series of disguises that distract the audience from Bruce Lee's absence.

Clips from *The Chinese Connection* and *Return of the Dragon* helped filmmakers complete the illusion of a true Bruce Lee movie. One scene even shows a life-size photo of Bruce Lee's head placed on top of a look-alike's body in a mirror. Because of scenes like these, and the small amount of footage that features the real Bruce Lee, many movie fans do not count *Game of Death* as an authentic Bruce Lee film.

ACTION HEROES

There will never be another Bruce Lee, but he paved the way for action stars around the world who followed in his footsteps. Audiences that were thrilled by Bruce Lee's fighting sequences later flocked to see stars like Chuck Norris, Arnold Schwarzenegger, and Jean-Claude Van Damme. The roots of their action movies clearly lie in the man-to-man combat sequences in Bruce Lee's films.

One of the most successful stars since Bruce Lee followed in the master's footsteps but created an action

Bruce helped pave the way for action stars like Jean-Claude Van Damme, right, *shown here in the 1988 film* Bloodsport.

genre all his own. Jackie Chan got his start as a Hong Kong movie stuntman. As a young man, Chan had received a solid thrashing from the furious fists of Bruce Lee in *Enter the Dragon.* In a brief sequence, Chan, dressed in the brown uniform of the villain Han's underground guards, has a lethal run-in with Lee. The master martial artist pulls the guard's hair and traps him in an armlock before breaking his neck and hurling him off the screen.

Chan started his rigorous training as a seven-year-old at the Peking Opera Academy and became skilled at both kung fu and acrobatics. What makes Chan unique and not just another Lee wannabe, is his reliance on humorous antics reminiscent of American silent film comics Charlie Chaplin and Buster Keaton.

In addition, Chan performs all of his death-defying stunts by himself. Outtakes appearing at the end of his movies often show Chan slamming into solid walls and even breaking his leg during one unsuccessful stunt.

Coincidentally, one of Chan's classmates at the Peking Opera Academy was Yuen Biao, who later performed acrobatic scenes as a double for Bruce Lee in *Game of Death*. Another of Chan's classmates, Sammo Hung, portraying a Shaolin Temple boxer, wrestles and loses to Bruce Lee in the dramatic opening of *Enter the Dragon*. This was the last fight scene Bruce ever made. Hung, who apparently appreciates large amounts of food, starred in a Hong Kong movie entitled *Enter the Fat Dragon* in 1978 and starred in the television series *Martial Law* in 1998.

As a young man, Jackie Chan, right, *had a brief encounter with Bruce Lee in the film* Enter the Dragon. *Chan has become successful with his unique combination of martial arts and humorous antics.*

From the time Brandon learned to walk, Bruce began to teach him the martial arts.

Chapter NINE

THE RISING SON

ALTHOUGH BRUCE LEE WAS NEVER REPLACED, SOME
fans had high hopes for the handsome young man
who carried on the Lee name. Bruce and Linda's son,
Brandon, combined the best of his dual heritage of
East and West. Although Brandon was born in California, he moved to Hong Kong with his family when
he was six. During the two years that they lived there,
he and his sister, Shannon, learned to speak fluent
Cantonese as well as English.

Brandon's famous father had groomed him for a future in the martial arts, training him to punch and
kick from the time he could walk. When he was just
five years old, Brandon impressed Hong Kong television audiences by smashing a wooden board with one

well-placed kick. Bruce taught Brandon the art of Jeet Kune Do and took him to martial arts tournaments where Bruce was giving demonstrations. As a seven-year-old, Brandon wrote an essay in school about his father, stating that he idolized him. When Bruce died, eight-year-old Brandon's life was shattered by the loss.

With Bruce gone, Linda decided to move back to California with Brandon and Shannon, then four years old. Losing his father was difficult enough for Brandon, but the move to the United States brought even more adjustments. In Hong Kong, he was used to his surroundings and most of his friends spoke Cantonese. Now he was in a new country, and everyone spoke English.

Linda, Brandon, and Bruce Lee

Fans of Bruce Lee's were hoping that Brandon, right, *could somehow fill the void left by Bruce's death.*

THE MAKING OF AN ACTOR

As Brandon grew up, his single desire was to become an actor. He majored in theater at Emerson College in Massachusetts and later studied acting in New York City and Los Angeles.

Ironically, in 1985, Brandon landed his first acting job in *Kung Fu: The Movie.* In this television role, he played the son of David Carradine, the man who years before had landed the starring role in television's long-running *Kung Fu* series. Brandon knew that his father had been denied the same part because of prejudice in Hollywood. If this seems strange, devoted *Green Hornet* fans were quick to point out that in one episode of the television series, "Alias the Scarf," Bruce had played opposite John Carradine—David Carradine's father.

Brandon, right, *choreographed and performed the electrifying fight sequences in the film* Rapid Fire.

Brandon wanted to succeed at acting without relying on his father's name, and he worked relentlessly to achieve this goal. He never wanted to be another Bruce Lee, he once explained, because even though he loved and admired his father, he was a totally different person who grew up in different surroundings and different times.

Yet when people heard that Brandon was the son of the great martial artist and actor, they had high hopes that he would fill the gap left by his father's death. Brandon had a hard time achieving his own artistic goals while living in the shadow of his father.

In 1988, Brandon starred in his first feature film,

Legacy of Rage, a movie produced in Hong Kong and filmed in Cantonese, which Brandon spoke fluently. The film was made for an Asian audience and played in the United States only in Chinese communities. Shortly after the release of *Legacy of Rage,* Brandon acted in another film, *Laser Mission,* shot in South Africa.

In 1991, the dashing young actor landed a major Hollywood role in *Showdown in Little Tokyo,* with Dolph Lundgren. The following year he gave an electrifying performance in *Rapid Fire,* for which he also choreographed the fight sequences.

Brandon once said that filming action scenes made him feel closer to his late father. Brandon sensed a new connection to Bruce because of the excitement both felt for the martial arts.

Brandon was offered an opportunity to portray his father in Dragon: The Bruce Lee Story *but turned it down. Jason Scott Lee,* below right, *played the part of Bruce Lee and Lauren Holly,* below left, *portrayed Linda in the 1992 film.*

Linda and Shannon Lee

Yet even though he loved and respected his late father, Brandon turned down a 1992 offer to portray the great martial artist in *Dragon: The Bruce Lee Story,* a movie loosely based on the life of Brandon's father. Brandon wanted to achieve fame in his own right and not be pegged as "just another Bruce Lee." Brandon's sister, Shannon, did contribute to the film, however. One scene of *Dragon: The Bruce Lee Story* includes her singing.

DRAGON LADY

ike her brother, Shannon Lee embodies the best of both American and Asian cultures. From age two to four, she lived in Hong Kong with her family. At nursery school, Shannon learned to speak Cantonese and to write Chinese characters. When her father passed away, she returned to California with her mother and brother. There, she attended American school during the week and Chinese school on Saturdays.

In college, at Tulane University in Louisiana, Shannon studied vocal performance, specifically opera. At her senior recital in 1991, she performed eleven songs in five different languages. Later, she sang in a scene from *Dragon: The Bruce Lee Story.*

Shannon studied Jeet Kune Do with her father's student Ted Wong, tae kwon do with Delon Tan, and kick boxing with Benny "The Jet" Urquidez. She continues to study wu shu with Eric Chen. Like her father and brother, Shannon became an actor. She appeared in the movies *Cage 2, High Voltage,* and *And Now You're Dead* in which she displays her talent for martial arts as well as acting.

Shannon is a mixture of East and West. When she smiles or takes a martial arts stance, you see a beautiful American woman with the soulful eyes and intensity of Bruce Lee.

THE CROW

Not wanting to be typecast as just an action hero, Brandon tried out for and landed the leading role in an eerie supernatural drama called *The Crow*. Based on James O'Barr's cult comic book, *The Crow* tells a dark, otherworldly tale about Eric Draven, a rock musician engaged to a woman named Shelly. Before they can get married, however, they are murdered. One

Brandon's role in the film The Crow *enabled him to show his dramatic acting talents.*

year after his death, Draven is brought back to life to wreak vengeance on his and his fiancée's killers.

The Crow was filmed at the Carolco studios in North Carolina in 1993. Somehow, the dark mood of the story transferred to the set, and the filming was plagued by odd accidents. A carpenter working on the production was nearly electrocuted by a live wire. Later that night, a truck used by the film crew accidentally burst into flames. What's more, an angry sculptor on the set deliberately smashed his car into some of the sculpted props, one worker seriously injured his hand with a screwdriver, and a severe storm ravaged the set of the dark drama.

Despite all the setbacks, the six-foot, one hundred sixty-pound Brandon put every ounce of his energy into what he called his best acting role. He was thrilled that the film would show his dramatic talents without the action scenes that some audiences expected from the son of Bruce Lee.

A SENSELESS TRAGEDY

These were good times for twenty-eight-year-old Brandon Lee. He was finally coming into his own fame as a serious actor, and he looked forward to marrying the love of his life, Eliza Hutton. They scheduled the happy event for April 17, 1993, one week after *The Crow's* expected completion. They rented out an entire hotel in Mexico for their guests and planned to charter a bus to take them to the celebration.

But on March 31, 1993, all of Brandon's blissful plans and future fame were destroyed by a freak accident. Just one week before filming was to finish, shortly after midnight, the crew assembled to film the scene in which Eric Draven is shot with a .44-caliber revolver.

Movie sequences such as this are shot with blanks, which give the illusion of real gunfire. In addition, Brandon was ready with a squib, a device that would set off a small explosion. It would mimic the action of a real bullet tearing through a bag of groceries in Brandon's arms.

The actor playing the murderer pointed the gun at Brandon. A shot rang out, and Brandon slumped in a corner, just as planned.

Yet something was wrong. Brandon didn't get up off the floor when the scene ended. Crew members ran to his side and discovered he was bleeding heavily from a wound in his abdomen. He was rushed to New Hanover Regional Medical Center, where a fragment of a bullet was found lodged against his spine.

A senseless and freak accident had occurred. A piece of a real bullet had accidentally remained in the revolver after a previous scene had been filmed. When the actor pulled the trigger, no one knew that a real piece of metal would shoot out with almost the same force as a whole bullet.

Intensive surgery could not repair the massive damage to Brandon's body and compensate for the loss of

Bruce and Brandon Lee are buried next to each other in Seattle's Lake View Cemetery.

blood. At 1:30 in the afternoon, twenty-eight-year-old Brandon Bruce Lee died. Like his father, Brandon died just before the release of his greatest movie.

On April 3, 1993, Linda Lee bravely but sadly stood at the site of her late husband's grave as Brandon Bruce Lee was laid to rest in Seattle's Lake View Cemetery next to his father. A stone bench in front of both gravestones bears the inscription, "The key to immortality is first living a life worth remembering."

REVIVED RUMORS

The wild theories that had circulated when Bruce Lee died in 1973 were revived when his son passed away. Reporters wondered in print whether there was a curse upon the men in the Lee family. They pointed out the strange similarity between Brandon's shocking death and a scene in *Game of Death,* in which Billy Lo is accidentally shot on a movie set. They brought back old rumors that Chinese criminals had killed both father and son.

The producers of *The Crow* had a serious decision on their hands. Should they scrap the movie altogether or piece together new footage without Brandon and complete the film? After consulting with Brandon's fiancée and his mother, producers decided that since this role had meant so much to Brandon, and since most of his scenes had already been filmed, the movie should be finished. The footage of the fatal shooting was removed from the film and destroyed. With a little rewriting and the latest in computer special effects, *The Crow* was completed.

Seven new scenes were created by computer. In some scenes, Brandon's face was digitally placed on the body of another actor. One scene, shot on a dark rainy night when Brandon was alive, was digitally manipulated into something totally new. In the original scene, Brandon appears in the background. In the computer-generated scene, the rain and darkness are removed, and Brandon appears in bright daylight. He is also moved to the foreground, with a new background behind him created by computer. When finally finished and released, *The Crow* attracted huge audiences, eager to see Brandon Lee in his last role.

EPILOGUE

On July 20, 1998, a quiet, unannounced group of family, friends, and fans gathered at the grave site of Bruce Lee at Lake View Cemetery in Seattle. The day was sunny, and a feeling of celebration and remembrance, not sadness, filled the air.

Linda Lee Cadwell, since remarried, read the same eulogy, or speech of praise, that she had read twenty-five years earlier when her husband passed away. She explained that Bruce had seen all human beings as united—despite race, religion, and nationality—and

In July 1998, Linda stood in front of friends and family and read the same eulogy she had read at Bruce's funeral twenty-five years earlier.

that he had urged all people to see the precious value of life in each waking moment. She said that Bruce had viewed every day of his short life as an opportunity for discovery. And rather than imitating others, Bruce had believed that the true meaning of life was found within.

"If you believe as I do that energy never disappears, but is merely transformed," Linda said, "then the energy that was Bruce continues to revitalize our spirits, unceasingly urging us to realize our talents through the path of self-knowledge."

Young and old alike still reap lessons from Bruce Lee, a seemingly ordinary man whose willpower, discipline, and focus allowed him to achieve the extraordinary. He was a man who took pride in perfection, adapted to new obstacles as they appeared, and learned new lessons every day of his short life.

He worked hard to bridge the gap between East and West, giving hope to oppressed people everywhere by showing them how to believe in themselves. The art of Jeet Kune Do, which he created, continues to build confidence and harmony in its practitioners.

As Linda Lee Cadwell reminded her listeners in the bright sunshine in the peaceful cemetery, "The light of stars that were extinguished years ago still reaches us. So it is with great men who died centuries ago, but still reach us with the radiation of their personality, and so it will be with Bruce . . . and will continue to be through the windows of time."

Sources

26   From Bruce Lee's handwritten essay, "A Moment of Understanding."

27   Ibid.

27   Ibid.

27   Bruce Lee, *The Ted Thomas Interview*, 1971. © 1995 Little-Wulff Creative Group.

31   Skip Ellsworth, telephone interview by the author, September 15, 1998.

32   Ibid.

32   Ibid.

32   Taky Kimura, interview by the author, July 19, 1998.

32–33   Ellsworth interview.

33   James DeMile, telephone interview by the author, September 21, 1998.

34   Ibid.

34   Ibid.

36   Taky Kimura interview.

46   Linda Lee Cadwell, interview by the author, February 11, 1999.

47   Linda Lee Cadwell, telephone interview by the author, September 11, 1998.

49   Linda Lee Cadwell, interview by the author, February 4, 1999.

70   Paul Heller, telephone interview by the author, September 10, 1998.

73   Michael Allin, interview by the author, August 17, 1998.

74   Heller interview.

PRONUNCIATION GUIDE

Bolo Yeung	BOH-LOH YUHNG
Cheng	CHEHNG
Chi Hon Tsoi	CHEE hahn SOY
Confucianism	kuhn-FYOO-shuh-nihzm
hapkido	HAHP-KEE-DOH
Kai Tak	KYE tahk
Krishnamurti	krihsh-nuh-MOOR-tee
Lee Heung Ying	HYOONG ying
Lee Hoi Chuen	HOY CHEHN
Lee Siu Lung	say-oo LUHNG
mah-jongg	MAH-ZHONG
Mo Si Ting	MOH see TIHNG
nunchaku	nuhn-CHAH-koo
Okinawan hapkido	OH-kihn-OW-ihn HAHP-KEE-DOH
pagoda	puh-GOH-duh
Sai Fon	SAH-EE FAHN
Shaolin	SHAH-OO-lihn
Shih Kien	shih KEEN
Sifu	SEE-foo
Taky Kimura	TAH-kee kih-MOOR-uh
Tang Lung	TAHNG luhng
Wong Fei Hung	WONG fay HUHNG
Yang Sze	YANG SEE

BIBLIOGRAPHY

BOOKS

Bruce Lee: The Untold Story. Burbank, CA: CFW Enterprises, 1986.

Chunovic, Louis. *Bruce Lee: The Tao of the Dragon Warrior.* New York: St. Martin's Griffin, 1996.

Clouse, Robert. *Bruce Lee: The Biography.* Burbank, CA: Unique Publications, 1988.

Clouse, Robert. *The Making of Enter the Dragon.* Burbank, CA: Unique Publications, 1987.

Corcoran, John, Emil Farkas, and Stuart Sobel. *The Original Martial Arts Encyclopedia: Tradition—History—Pioneers.* Los Angeles: Pro-Action Publishing, 1993.

Costa, Shu Shu. *Lotus Seeds and Lucky Stars: Asian Myths and Traditions about Pregnancy and Birthing.* New York: Simon & Schuster, 1998.

Dear Bruce Lee. Santa Clarita, CA: Ohara Publications, Inc., 1980.

DeMile, James. *Bruce Lee's 1 and 3 Inch Power Punch.* Quilcene, WA: Tao of Wing Chun Do Publications, 1997.

Gaul, Lou. *The Fist That Shook the World: The Cinema of Bruce Lee.* Baltimore: Midnight Marquee Press, Inc., 1997.

Lawlor, Jennifer. *The Martial Arts Encyclopedia.* Indianapolis: Masters Press, 1996.

Lee, Bruce. *Jeet Kune Do: Bruce Lee's Commentaries on the Martial Way.* Edited by John Little. North Clarendon, VT: Charles E. Tuttle Co., Inc., 1997.

Lee, Bruce. *The Tao of Gung Fu: A Study in the Way of Chinese Martial Art.* Edited by John Little. North Clarendon, VT: Charles E. Tuttle Co., Inc., 1997.

Lee, Bruce. *Tao of Jeet Kune Do.* Santa Clarita, CA: Ohara Publications, Inc., 1975.

Lee, Bruce. *Words of the Dragon: Interviews 1958–1973.* Edited by John Little. North Clarendon, VT: Charles E. Tuttle Co., Inc., 1997.

Lee, Bruce, and M. Uyehara. *Bruce Lee's Fighting Method: Self-Defense Techniques.* Santa Clarita, CA: Ohara Publications, Inc., 1976.

Lee, Linda. *The Bruce Lee Story.* Santa Clarita, CA: Ohara Publications, Inc., 1989.

The Legendary Bruce Lee. By the editors of *Black Belt* magazine. Santa Clarita, CA: Ohara Publications, Inc., 1986.

Logan, Bey. *Hong Kong Action Cinema.* Woodstock, NY: The Overlook Press, 1995.

Meyers, Richard, Amy Harlib, Bill Palmer, and Karen Palmer. *From Bruce Lee to the Ninjas: Martial Arts Movies.* New York: Carol Publishing Group, 1991.

Palmer, Bill, Karen Palmer, and Ric Meyers. The *Encyclopedia of Martial Arts Movies.* Metuchen, NJ: Scarecrow Press, 1995.

Uyehara, M. *Bruce Lee: The Incomparable Fighter.* Santa Clarita, CA: Ohara Publications, Inc., 1988.

Magazine and Newspaper Articles

"Bruce Lee, 32, Star of Kung Fu Movies." Obituary, *New York Times,* July 21, 1973.

"Bruce Lee: The Way of the Dragon." *Martial Arts Legends,* December 1995.

Ochs, Phil. "Requiem for a Dragon Departed." *Time Out,* February 15–21, 1974.

"Screaming Fans Mob Kung Fu Star's Funeral." *New York Post,* July 25, 1973.

Sharkey, Betsy. "Fate's Children: Bruce and Brandon Lee." *New York Times,* May 2, 1993.

Topor, Tom. "Kung Fu: Box Office Smash." *New York Post,* May 10, 1973.

FILMOGRAPHY

From 1946 to 1958, Bruce Lee appeared as a child actor in twenty Hong Kong movies in comic and tragic roles.

Feature Films

Marlowe (small part, shown in brief fighting scene) 1969

Fists of Fury 1971
(Asian title: *The Big Boss*)

The Chinese Connection 1972
(Asian title: *Fist of Fury*)

Return of the Dragon 1972
(Asian title: *Way of the Dragon*)

Began filming *Game of Death*, 1972, which contains only short sequences of the real Bruce Lee. It was completed in 1978 with stand-ins after his death.

Enter the Dragon 1973

Television Roles

The Green Hornet 1966–1967

Bit parts in three television shows: *Blondie, Ironside,* and *Here Come the Brides* 1968–1969

Fight Coordinator

A Walk in the Spring Rain 1969
The Wrecking Crew 1969

INDEX

Bruce prepares to fight with a nanchaku in each hand from this scene in Way of the Dragon.

FOR MORE INFORMATION

For more information on Bruce Lee and Jun Fan Jeet Kune Do, contact:

Jun Fan Jeet Kune Do
    Nucleus
P. O. Box 1390
Clovis, CA 93613-1390
(209) 298-5553
www.jkd.com

For information on efforts to continue the Bruce and Brandon Lee legacy, contact:

Bruce Lee and Brandon Lee
    Medical Scholarship
    Endowment
University of Arkansas
4301 West Markham #716
Little Rock, AK 72205-7199
(501) 686-7950

Brandon Bruce Lee Drama
    Scholarship
Whitman College
Development Office
Walla Walla, WA 99362
(509) 527-5165

PHOTO ACKNOWLEDGMENTS

Photographs are reproduced with the permission of: Everett Collection, back cover, p. 2; Photofest, pp. 6, 44, 59, 62, 64, 71, 88, 109 (top); Grant Smith/Corbis, pp. 10, 18; Private Collection of Linda Lee Cadwell, pp. 12, 17, 20, 23, 25, 26, 29, 49, 86; Minneapolis Institute of Arts, p. 14; Archive Photos, pp. 30, 43; The Kobal Collection, pp. 33, 53, 61, 82, 92, 106; Globe Photos, pp. 34, 50, 75, 78, 89, 109 (bottom); Doris Nieh/Globe Photos, pp. 36, 84; JBP/Globe Photos, p. 39; UPl/Corbis-Bettmann, pp. 40, 45, 56; John Springer/Corbis-Bettmann, p. 66; © Jeffrey Mayer/Star File, p. 83; Luke Wynne/The Kobal Collection, p. 87; © Michael Ferguson/Globe Photos, p. 90; Linda Tagliaferro, pp. 95, 98; Steve Eisenberg, p. 112.

Cover photos
Hardcover: Everett Collection
Softcover: S.S. Archives/Shooting Star

OTHER TITLES FROM LERNER AND A&E®:

ABOUT THE AUTHOR

Linda Tagliaferro is a writer and illustrator whose previous books include *Genetic Engineering: Progress or Peril?* and *Destination New York.*

Linda is a regular contributor to the *New York Times,* and she has written for numerous newspapers and magazines. She was born in Brooklyn, New York, and has lived and studied in Denmark, Italy, and Indonesia. She lives in Little Neck, New York, with her husband and teenage son.

Author's Note: I would like to thank Linda Lee Cadwell for her generous help with this book. In addition, I would like to thank Seaton Chang; Lisa Rowland, her husband, and especially her cats; Taky Kimura; Skip Ellsworth; Jim DeMile; John Little; Michael Allin; Paul Heller; Ric Meyers; Dave Cater; Charles Silver and Ron Megliosi of the Film Study Center at the Museum of Modern Art, New York City; the staff at the Museum of Television and Radio, New York City; my husband, Fred Thorner, and my son, Eric Thorner, for putting up with all those kung fu movies; the staff at Lerner Publications and A&E Television Networks; Ken Sang from the Hong Kong Tourist Association; and everyone else who made this book possible.